2000 STICKERS EMOTICON

PaRragon

Bath • New York • Cologne • Melbourne • Delhi
Hong Kong • Shenzhen • Singapore

Express Yourself

From happy to sad and everything in between – there's a smiley to match every mood! These little faces will help you express yourself and understand how others are feeling, too.

Do you know your smileys? Add the missing letters.

Sad

imbarrissed

Sleepy

angry

amused

grinning

Lovin' it

Sneaky

Horried

Scarey

Surprised

Sick

cool

air

crying

angelic

m_h

happy

Laughing

_eliev_d

bored

t_arf_l

Translate each text message into a smiley.

Feeling kinda tired.

Done all my chores!

W-w-what was that?

Phew! That was close.

That rocks!

LOL! Soooo funny.

Me, Me, Me!

Fill in the blanks using words and emoticons.

My name is: _Molly Nora copelin_

I'm _8_ years old.

My birthday is: _14th August_

My mood today is:

The weather today is:

I love to eat:

My best sports are:

My fave animals are:

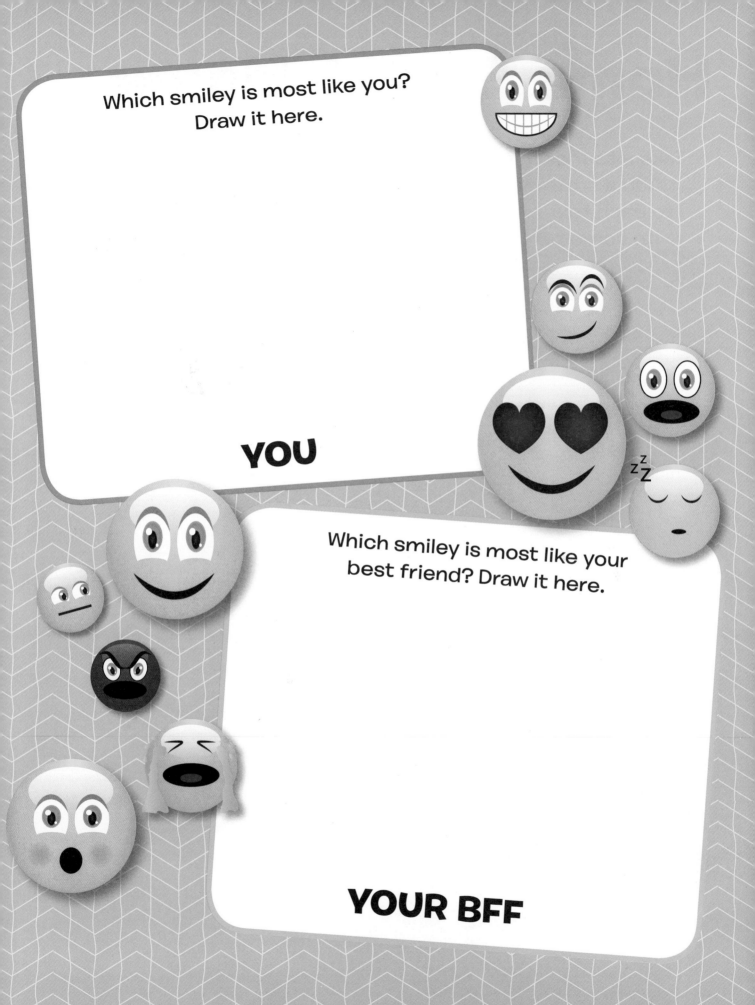

Which smiley is most like you?
Draw it here.

YOU

Which smiley is most like your
best friend? Draw it here.

YOUR BFF

Home Sweet Home

Take a tour of this cool house! Add a smiley sticker next to each text message, then write some texts of your own.

Ugh! I need some fresh air!

Now where did I leave my shoes?

Funny Feelings

Say what? Draw lines to match each smiley to its speech bubble.

1 Zzz! I need my bed.

2 LOL! You crack me up!

3 I don't **feel** too good!

4 Whhaatt! No way!

5 LOVE IT!

A

B

C

D

E

6

I can't believe I just called my teacher "mum"!

F

7

Looking **good,** feeling **good.**

G

8

Grr! Who ate my doughnut?

H

Use your smiley stickers to fill in the blanks.

embarrassed

sleepy

crying

angry

grinning

laughing

lovin' it

happy

cool

worried

surprised

sick

sneaky

Oddballs

Which smiley is different from the rest? Circle the odd one out on each screen.

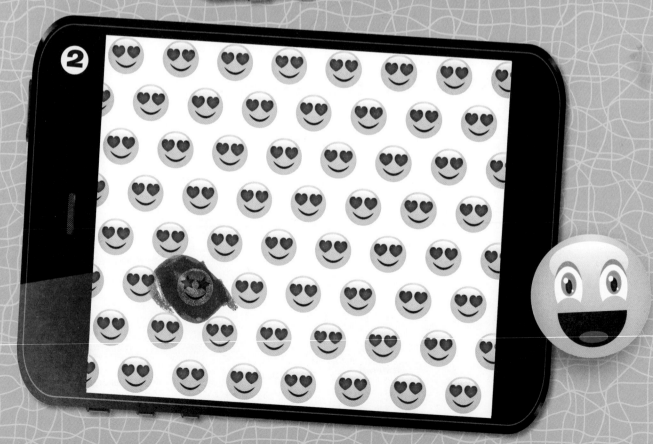

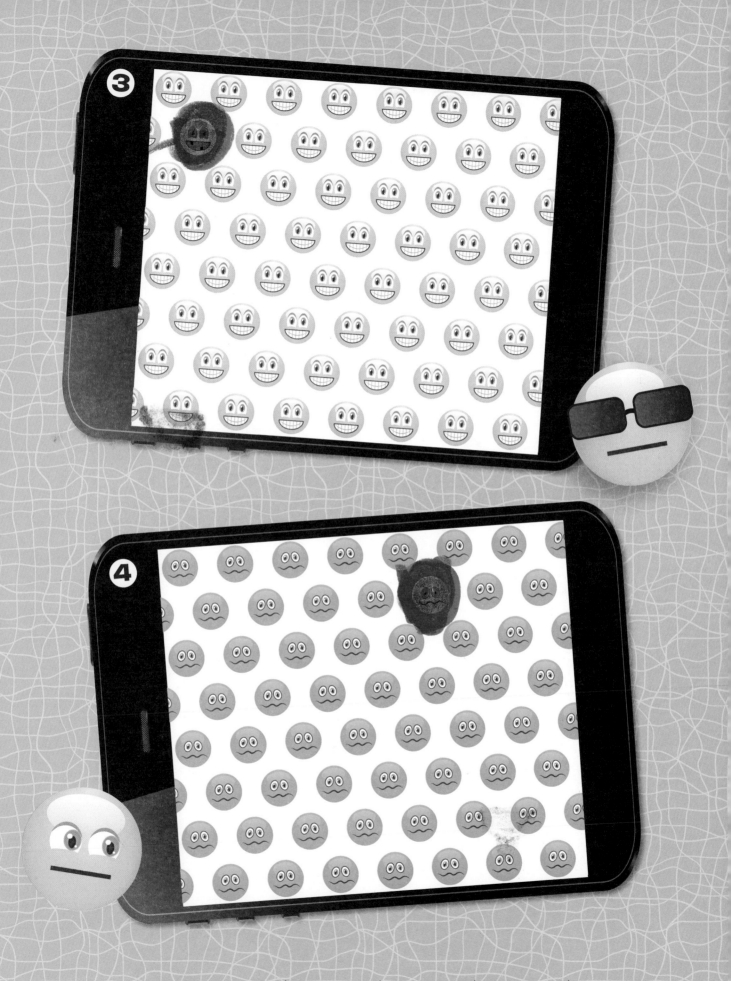

New Look

Grab your stickers and get creative —
give each smiley an epic new look.

Add hats, moustaches, glasses — whatever you like!

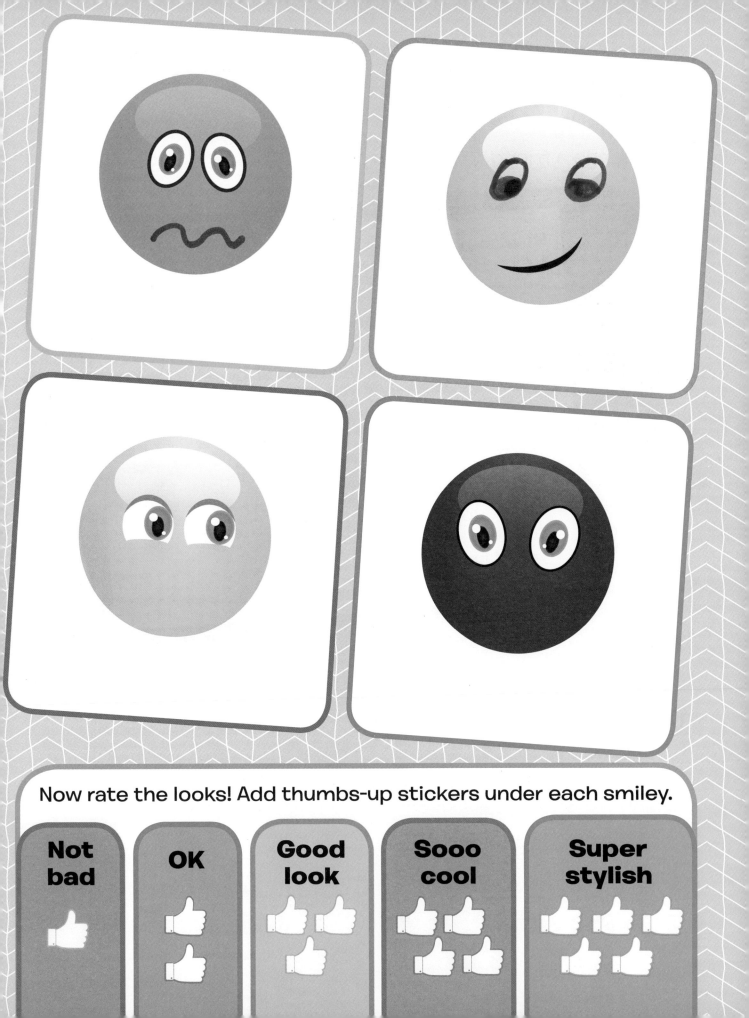

Now rate the looks! Add thumbs-up stickers under each smiley.

Not bad

OK

Good look

Sooo cool

Super stylish

Naughty and Nice

Challenge a friend to play this game of good and bad!

How to play:

1 Find the naughty and nice stickers.

2 Flip a coin to see who'll be naughty and who'll be nice!

3 The nice smiley starts the first game!

4 Each player in turn places a sticker in any of the squares in the grid.

5 To win the game, simply make a row of three naughty or nice smileys.

6 Write the winner's name under each completed game.

7 Play the best of seven games, then count up the names to reveal the true pro player!

Good luck!

Rows can be horizontal, vertical or diagonal!

1

2

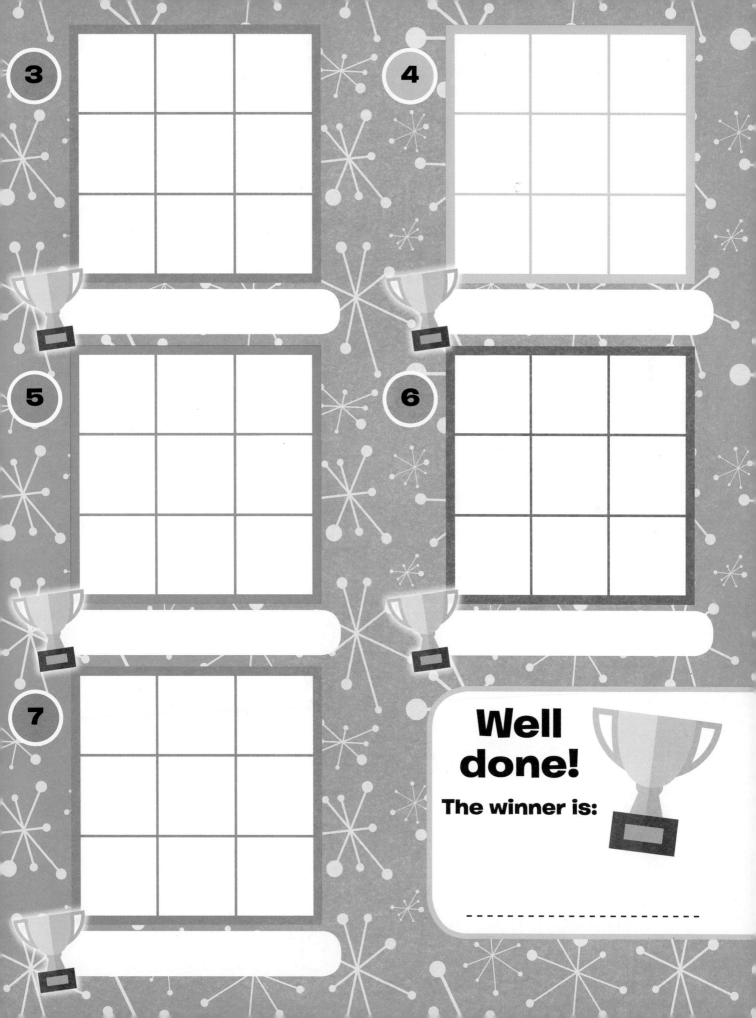

Well done!

The winner is:

- -

Make Some Noise!

Let's rock! Add a smiley sticker next to each text message, then write some musical texts of your own.

I'm a star on my **guitar!**

Hey, **Mr DJ!**

I can't stop whistling!
Turn the radio up to LOUD!
I never miss a beat!

Who's Texting?

Who's messaging who? Match each phone on the left with its partner on the right.

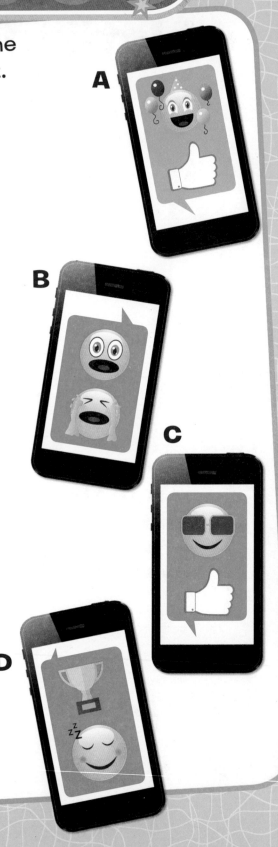

Deep Thinker

What's on your mind? Say it in emoticons! Draw or use stickers to show what you are thinking about.

Gridlock

Use your stickers to complete the grids so that each row and column contains these smileys:

1

2

3

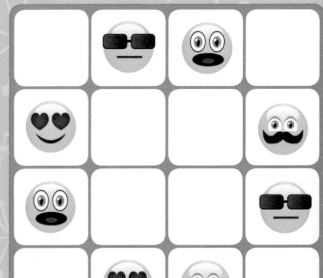

Which Words?

Think of five different words to describe each smiley,
then write the words in the columns below.

All Seasons

Send a text for every season! Mix words and stickers to make your message. Finish the first message, then create three more.

In a Tangle

What a tangled ball of emotions! Follow the lines to reveal how the girl is feeling.

Hidden Picture

Colour in the
shapes using
the colour
code to reveal
a hidden smiley.

What would make
you feel like this?

_____

_____

_____

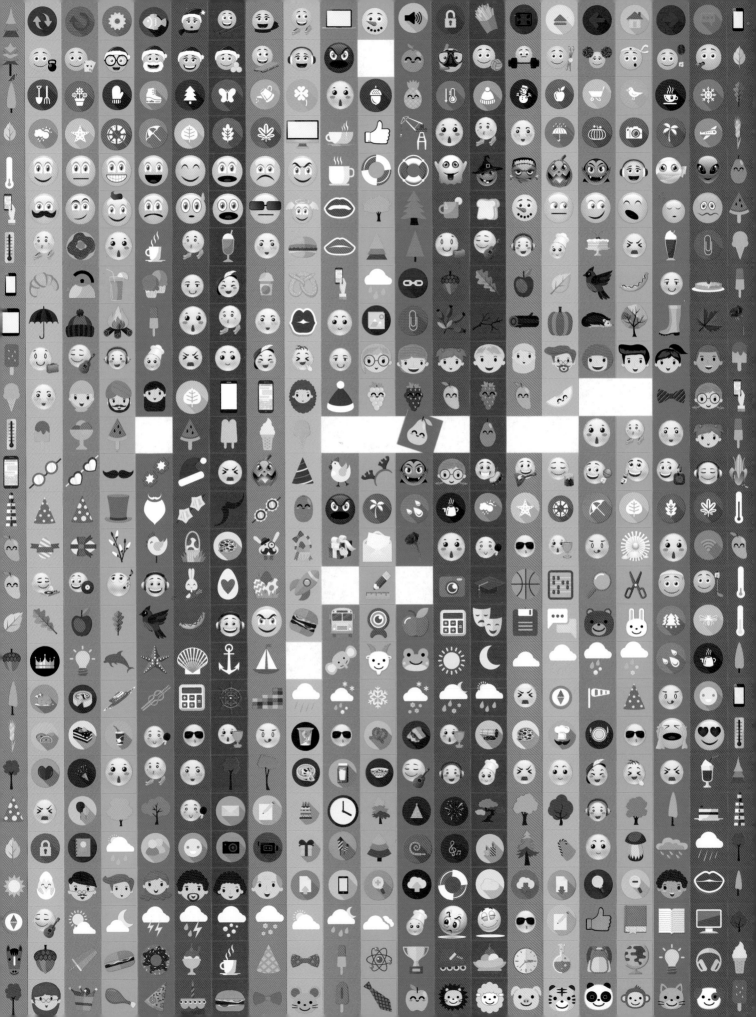

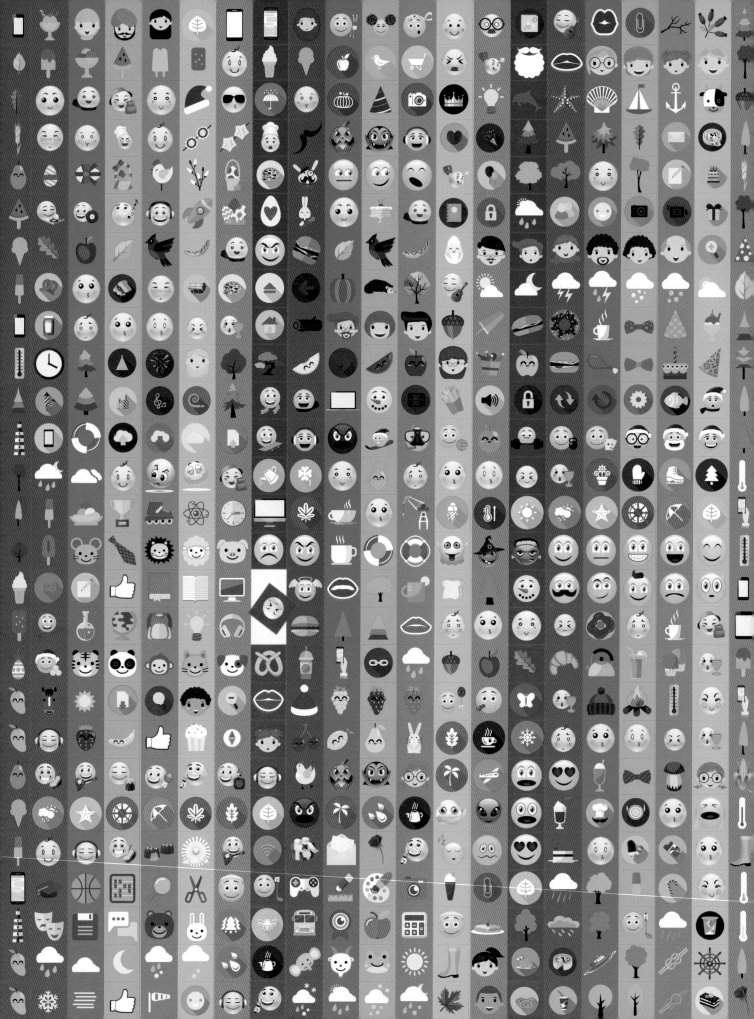

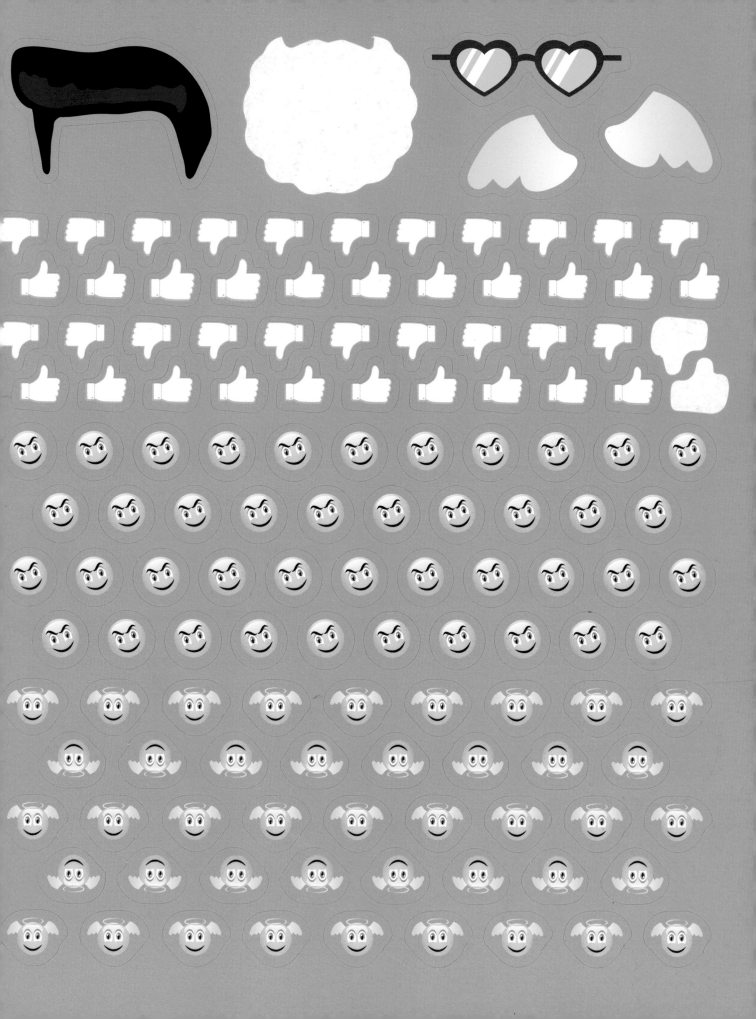

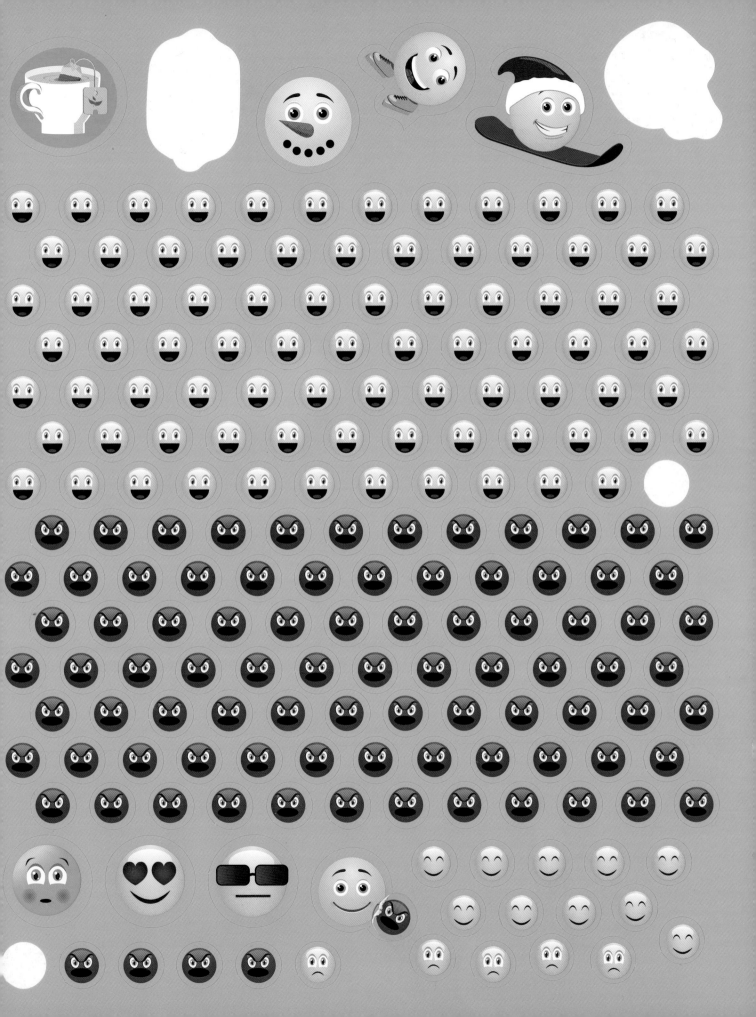

Stick 'Em Up!

Which emoticons are missing from each row?
Use your stickers to fill in the blanks.

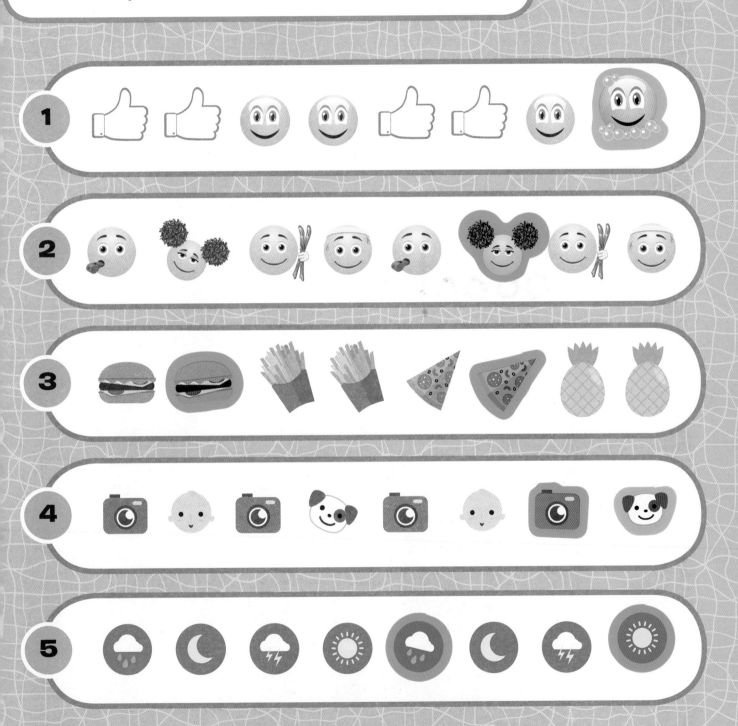

It's Halloween, and everyone's feeling spooky! Add a smiley sticker next to each text message, then write some spooky texts of your own.

booo!

I wanna go **home!**

Trick or **Treat?**

What's the Story?

Translate these emoticon stories into words!

Now make up your own story using any stickers you like!

Totally You!

Try this fun quiz to discover which smiley best matches your personality. Tick **A**, **B** or **C** each time!

Which fancy dress costume suits you best?  **A** ✓  **B** ☐  **C** ☐

What type of holiday would you rather take?  **A** ☐ 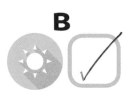 **B** ✓  **C** ☐

Which subject do you enjoy most at school? 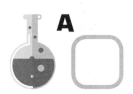 **A** ☐  **B** ☐ 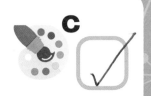 **C** ✓

What colour suits you?  **A** ☐ **B** ☐ 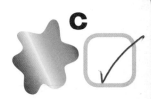 **C** ✓

Which day of the year do you most enjoy? 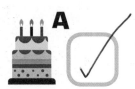 **A** ✓ **B** ✓  **C** ☐

Which fruit would you snack on?

A ✓ B ☐ C ☐

How do you like to chill out?

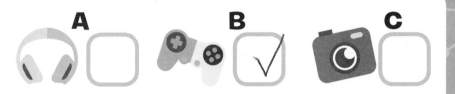

A ☐ B ✓ C ☐

Which animal would make the cutest pet?

A ✓ B ☐ C ☐

Which is your fave flavour?

A ✓ B ☐ C ☐

Mostly As

You're super cool and brilliantly brainy. You keep calm even when friends and family get in a fluster. A smart cookie.

Mostly Bs

You're a positive, happy-go-lucky person. You get along well with all sorts of people thanks to your friendly, sunny nature!

Mostly Cs

You're curious, creative and brave enough to do your own thing. It's much more exciting than following the crowd!

Eyes Peeled!

These emoticon messages have been hidden in the grid. Try to find them as quickly as you can. The messages are written up, down, forwards, backwards and diagonally.

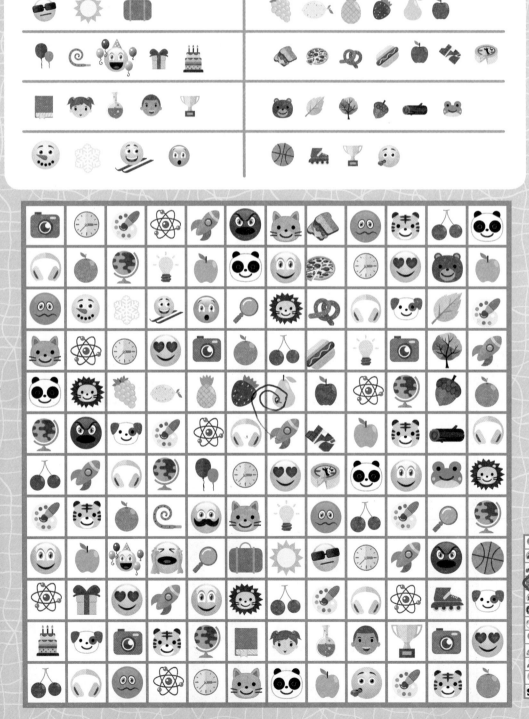

Memory Game

Feeling hungry? Study these food and drink emoticons for 60 seconds, then turn the page and try to remember as many as you can.

Memory Game

How many tasty treats were on the previous page? Find stickers of all the emoticons you can remember... without peeking!

Opposites Attract

Draw a line to match each smiley to its opposite.

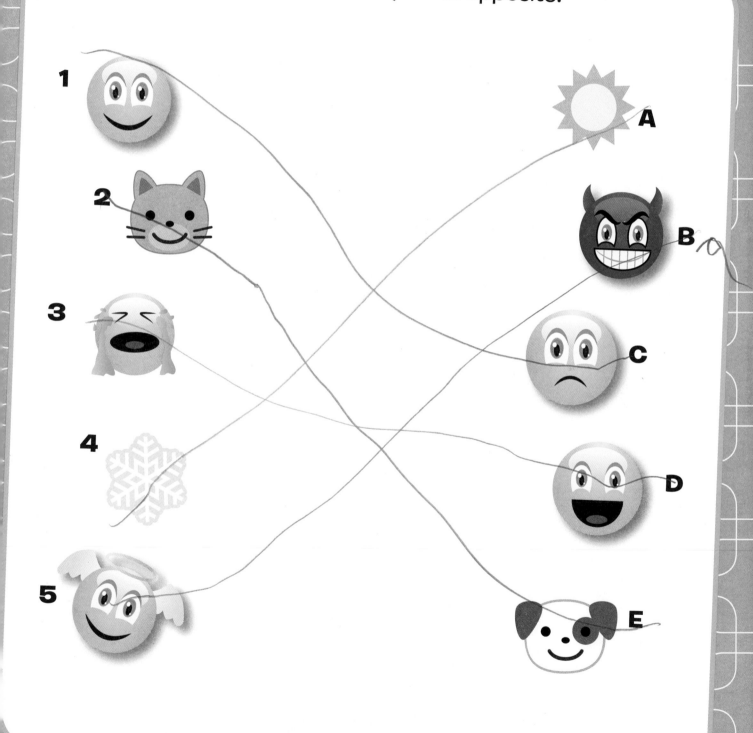

1

2

3

4

5

A

B

C

D

E

Feeling Frosty

Brr! Winter has arrived. Add a smiley sticker next to each text message, then write some snowy texts of your own.

I'm a **super** snowboarder!

Join me for a **snowball fight!**

I've lost my **head!**

I'm **great** on **skates!**

Tell the Future

You don't need a crystal ball to tell the future! Make this cool fortune teller, then predict what's in store for a friend!

1

Fold a square of paper in half from corner to corner, to make a triangle shape.

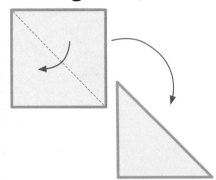

2

Fold the paper in half again, making a smaller triangle.

3

Unfold the paper to reveal an 'X' crease.

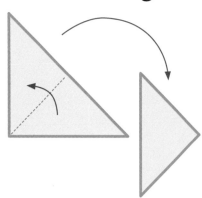

4

Fold one corner of the paper to the centre of the square (the middle point of the X), then repeat with the other three corners.

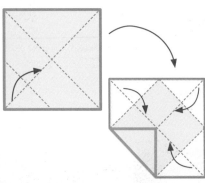

5

You should end up with a smaller square — flip this over.

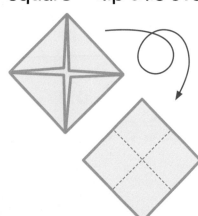

6

Fold one corner to the centre of the square (the middle point of the X), then repeat with the other three corners. You'll end up with an even smaller square!

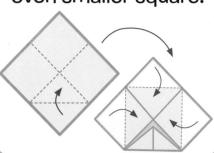

7

Fold and unfold the bottom edge of the square up to the top edge.

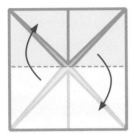

8

Fold and unfold the left edge of the square across to the right edge.

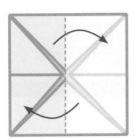

9

Place your fingers under the flaps of the fortune teller, so you move the four quarters back and forth.

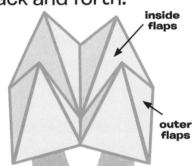

inside flaps

outer flaps

10

Choose four colours for the outer flaps. Write numbers 1 to 8 on the inside flaps. Underneath the numbered flaps, write some fortunes and add smiley stickers to match.

Maybe you'll be happy, rich, well-travelled or super stylish! **You choose!**

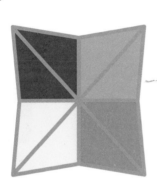

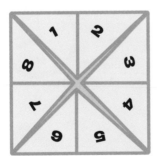

How to play:

1 Ask a friend to pick one of the four colours. Spell out the colour, opening and closing the fortune teller for each letter. For example: b l u e (four times).

2 Ask a friend how old they are. Count out the number, opening and closing the fortune teller for each number.

3 Ask a friend to pick a number from 1 to 8. Lift the same-numbered flap to reveal your friend's fortune!

Picture This

Have you tried messaging friends ONLY using emoticons?
Match each text message to its emoticon version,
then see how well you scored.

1 YAY! Mum and Dad are home!

2 I'm so sorry.

3 LOL! I'm crying with laughter!

4 I love, love, love dogs!

5 Time to party!

6 You go, girl!

 **A**

 **B**

 **C**

 **D**

 **E**

 **F**

7 Time for **pizza?**

 G

8 Just **joking!**

 H

9 Selfie with my **kitty!**

I

10 Ahh, a cool drink of **milk.**

J

11 **Goodnight,** sleep tight.

K

12 Did I really just **say that?**

   L

9-12 correct answers
Wow! Epic emoticons! You rock!

4-8 correct answers
You know your emoticons! Good stuff!

0-3 correct answers
Oops! Try again to boost your score.

Four in a Row

Challenge a friend to see who'll be the first to stick four in a row!

How to play:
1. Find the happy and angry stickers.
2. Flip a coin to see who'll be happy and who'll be angry!
3. The happy smiley starts the first game!
4. Each player in turn places a sticker at the bottom of a column.
5. To win the game, simply make a row of four happy or angry smileys.
6. Write the winner's name next to each completed game.
7. Play the best of three games, then count up the names to reveal who's the champion!

Good luck!

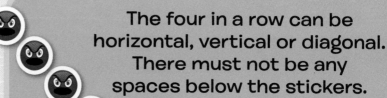

The four in a row can be horizontal, vertical or diagonal. There must not be any spaces below the stickers.

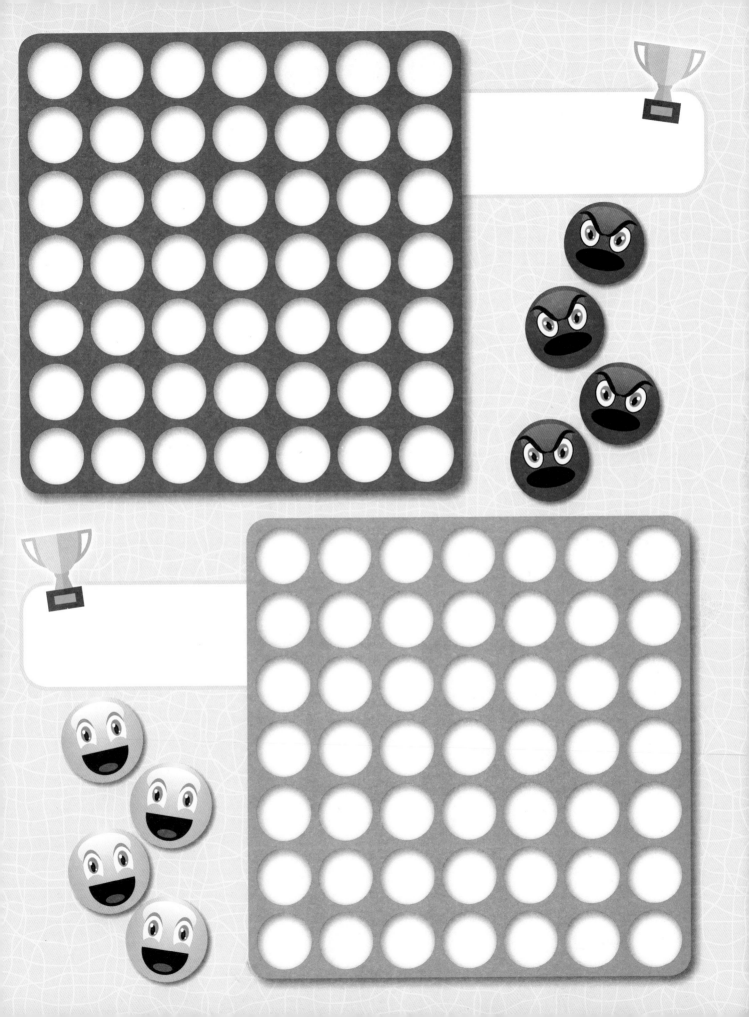

Hit the Beach

School's out for the summer! Add a smiley sticker next to each text message, then write some sunny texts of your own.

Too much sun! Oww!

I love sunny days!

Seeing Red?

Do you try to stay positive when things aren't going your way? Read the statements, then add a smiley sticker next to the happy action each time!

1 You auditioned for the lead role in the school play, but your best friend bagged the part...

A ◯ Grr! The play sucks anyway!

B ◯ My BFF will be awesome! I can't wait to watch the play!

2 You're out shopping when a sudden shower soaks you...

A ◯ Great! I love dancing in the rain!

B ◯ Just my luck.

3 It's your fave chocolate cake for dessert at lunch, but you're last in the queue...

A ◯ If I don't get a slice, everyone's going to know about it!

B ◯ No problem — I'll choose another tasty treat instead.

4 You feel wiped out and full of germs...

A ◯ A day snuggling on the sofa might be just what the doctor ordered.

B ◯ Ugh! Why does this always happen to me?

5 You start a new dance class, but no one you know shows up...

A ◯ I won't be going back next week.

B ◯ If I smile and be friendly, maybe I'll make some new friends.

Got the Blues?

When you're feeling sad and blue, take action to turn that frown upside down! Add a smiley sticker next to the happy action each time!

1 Your little brother rips a cool picture you painted...

A ⃝ I'll never be able to paint one as good again.

B ⃝ No worries — my next painting will be a real masterpiece!

2 Your team lost in the final of a big competition...

A ⃝ We'll look at what went wrong together and train extra hard next time.

B ⃝ We lost. I feel rubbish. Maybe I should quit the team.

3 Your fave T-shirt got shrunk in the wash, and it's too tiny to wear...

A ⃝ Sob! It went with ALL my outfits.

B ⃝ Never mind — my little cousin will love it!

4 It's the school holidays, but your best friend has gone on holiday...

A ⃝ I'll miss my BFF so much! These holidays are going to be so boring.

B ⃝ I'll plan things to do each day, so we'll have loads to talk about when my buddy is back.

5 A big test at school is making you worry...

A ⃝ I'll cheer myself up by chilling with a book or watching TV. Worrying won't help.

B ⃝ I can't do this! I'm sure to fail.

On Screen

There are five differences between these two text messages. Circle the differences as you find each one.

goodbye!

bye!

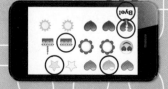